Grandmother's Nursery Rhymes
Las Nanas de Abuelita

Grandmother's Nursery Rhymes

Lullabies,
Tongue Twisters, and Riddles
from South America

Canciones de cuna,
trabalenguas y adivinanzas
de Suramérica

Las Nanas de Abuelita

COMPILED BY/COMPILADO POR Nelly Palacio Jaramillo

ILLUSTRATED BY/ILUSTRADO POR Elivia

HENRY HOLT AND COMPANY · NEW YORK

"Mommy and Daddy,
I'd like a chance
to marry a girl
Who knows how to dance."

"Marry, my son
And we will give you
Brown dancing shoes
Shiny and new."

—Papá, mamá,
Me quiero casar
Con una niñita
Que sepa bailar.

—Cásate, cásate,
Que yo te daré
Zapatos y medias
De color café.

Sawdust, sawdust, over me
Loggers from across the sea
Ask for sweetbread
Ask for tea,
From afar,
Candy bars,
From nearby,
Chocolate pie,
From the fleet,
Trick or treat,
Trick or trick or trick or treat,
Trick or trick a treat.

A, E, I, O, U
A donkey knows much more than you!

A, E, I, O, U
¡El burro sabe más que tú!

The following rhymes are called adivinanzas.
These are riddles in which you try to guess the letter or the object.

I'm not a lighthouse or a rock,
But I live at the end of the sea,
You'll also find me in the sand:
Now guess who I might be.

Sin ser faro ni roca
En medio del mar estoy,
También estoy en la playa:
¡Adivinen, pues, quién soy!

a

Glory doesn't have it,
Nor the sky since the time of birth,
But God in his great wisdom
Gave it to the earth.

En la gloria no la hubo,
En el mundo no se halló,
Dios con ser Dios no la tuvo
Y al hombre Dios se la dio.

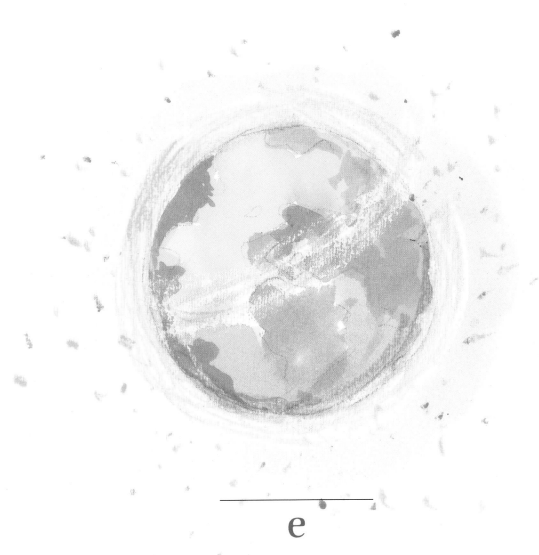

e

I'm a stick
Standing high
Above my head
There floats a fly.

Soy un palito
Muy derechito,
Sobre la frente
Llevo un mosquito.

i

I'm in the word of God,
I'm why the world is round,
I'm inside of every person
Who listens for my sound.

Soy la redondez de mundo,
Sin mí no puede haber Dios,
Papas, cardenales, sí,
Pero pontífices, no.

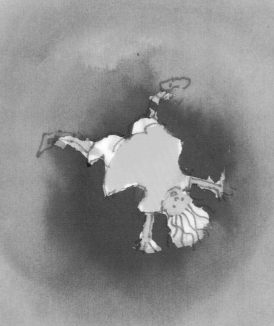

O

By a burro hauled
In a trunk of blue,
I don't have it, this I know,
But certainly you do!

La carga el burro,
La guarda el baúl,
Yo no la tengo
La tienes ¡tú!

u

One pretty lady,
Looking very rich,
Despite her coat of rags
She made without a stitch.

The Hen

Una señorita
Muy aseñorada,
Con muchos remiendos
Ni una puntada.

La gallina

In the air I play,
In the air I lurk,
In the air I weave,
In the air I work.

The Spider

En el aire anda,
En el aire mora,
En el aire teje
La trabajadora.

La araña

Although I have my legs,
I cannot move an inch.
Food that I can carry
I cannot even pinch.

The Table

A pesar de tener patas,
Yo no me puedo mover,
Llevo la comida encima
Y no la puedo comer.

La mesa

I whistle without lips,
I fly without wings,
I clap without hands
And touch all living things.

The Wind

Vuela sin alas,
Silba sin boca,
Azota sin manos,
Nadie lo toca.

El viento

Sprinklers that are bigger
Than the great, big sun,
Sprinkling the earth
Until the harvest's done.

The Clouds

Unas regaderas
Más grandes que el sol,
Con que riega el campo
Dios, nuestro Señor.

Las nubes

A little black cow
Went into the sea;
Neither captain nor sailor
Can bring her to me.

The Night

Una vaquita negra
Se entró al mar;
Capitán ni marinero
La podrá sacar.

La noche

Always quiet,
Always blinking,
By day sleeping,
At night winking.

The Stars

Siempre quietas,
Siempre inquietas,
Durmiendo de día,
De noche despiertas.

Las estrellas

"Dear Saint Anne, dear Saint Anne,
Why cries the child?"
"Because of an apple
He lost in the wild."

"If he cries for one,
I'll give him two,
One is for him
The other's for you."

"Saint Joseph, Saint Joseph,
Might I ask you?
Why cries the baby?
What can we do?"

"It's true, he is crying
This child we adore,
But soon he'll be sleeping—
Shh—hear his soft snore.

—Señora Santa Ana
¿por qué llora el niño?
—Por una manzana
Que se le ha perdido.

—Si llora por una
Yo le daré dos,
Una para el niño
Y otra para vos.

—Señor San José,
Señor San José,
¿por qué llora el niño
se puede saber?

—El niño bendito
llorando está,
Porque, mi chiquito,
No quiere roncar.

This pretty child
wants to sleep, wants to sleep.
Playful little dreams
Will not keep, will not keep.

Sleep, little child,
sleep, little you,
before the rooster wakes us
with a cock-a-doodle-doo.

Este niño lindo
se quiere dormir
y el pícaro sueño
no quiere venir.

Duerme, mi niño,
duérmete, tú,
antes que venga
el currucucú.

Grandfather's Poem

Little child, little sprite,
They painted your eyebrows
With a brush so slight,
And made your ears
From seashells white.
Who's the brightest?
White, white moon!
Who smells sweetest?
White, white flower!
Sleep, sleep, my little star,
You're my moon, my little flower,
Darling, darling, sleep and rest,
The sun has set far in the west.

Poema del Abuelo

Chiquita, cosita,
Te hicieron las cejas
Con una brochita,
Y las orejitas
Con un caracol.
¿Quién mas linda?
¡Blanca luna!
¿Quién más dulce?
¡Blanca flor!
Duerme, duérmete,
mi estrella,
Blanca Luna,
Blanca Flor,
Primor, primor,
duérmete, niña,
Que ya se fue el sol.

A mis hijos, Pablo y Raquel; a mis nietos
—N. P. J.

To Stanley, with love
—E.

Henry Holt and Company, LLC, *Publishers since 1866*, 115 West 18th Street, New York, New York 10011. Henry Holt is a registered trademark of Henry Holt and Company, LLC. Text copyright © 1994 by Nelly Palacio Jaramillo. Illustrations copyright © 1994 by Elivia Savadier. Translation copyright © by Raquel Jaramillo. All rights reserved. Distributed in Canada by H. B. Fenn and Company Ltd. Library of Congress Cataloging-in-Publication Data: Las Nanas de abuelita: canciones de cuna, trabalenguas y adivinanzas de Suramérica = Grandmother's nursery rhymes: lullabies, tongue twisters, and riddles from South America / compiled by Nelly Palacio Jaramillo; illustrated by Elivia Savadier. Summary: A collection of traditional South American nursery rhymes in both Spanish and English. 1. Nursery rhymes, Spanish American. 2. Nursery rhymes, Spanish American—Translations into English. 3. Riddles, Spanish American. 4. Riddles, Spanish American—Translations into English. 5. Riddles, Juvenile. [1. Nursery rhymes. 2. Spanish language materials—Bilingual.] I. Jaramillo, Nelly Palacio. II. Savadier, Elivia, ill. III. Title: Grandmother's nursery rhymes. PZ74.3.N34 1994 93-41363 / Printed in the United States of America on acid-free paper. ∞ The artist used water-soluble inks with pen on Fabriano watercolor paper to create the illustrations for this book.

First published in hardcover in 1994 by Henry Holt and Company
First Owlet paperback edition—1996

ISBN 0-8050-2555-3 (hardcover)
3 5 7 9 10 8 6 4
ISBN 0-8050-4644-5 (paperback)
9 10 8